To Flourish and Prosper.

A Book of Inspirational Poetry

By

R. Thomas McPherson

To Flourish and Prosper.
A Book of Inspirational Poetry
By
R. Thomas McPherson

Also by R Thomas McPherson

The Corporate Wars

Investigation

Insurrection

The Corporate Wars Vol 2

Inquisition

Inclusion

Incursion

Invasion

The Veterans of the Psychic Wars

Hostile Waters

Third Dawn

Identity Crisis

War Drums

Battle Cry

Queen's Gambit

Standalone

The Wastelands
The Corporate Wars
The Veterans of the Psychic Wars
The Veterans of the Psychic Wars Volume 2
To Flourish and Prosper.

Table of Contents

This Book is Dedicated to Shannon. She is the reason it was written.
She has been as inspiring to me as I hope I am to you.
I hope I can uplift your spirit and bring joy to your day.

To Flourish and Prosper.

It is an interesting concept, to win in the face of adversity.
To be ground into the mud by those who would call themselves family and friends. That is true adversity. It is man that is his own greatest enemy, and by chance, his own greatest ally.
For there are a few that do not wish to ground you into the mud, but to bring you into the light, clean you up, and make you shine bright.
You will fight them all the way feeling that you are not worthy. Those that have ground you into the mud have done their job well.
It has been my great honor to know such a person, and I hope with the most fervent wish that I can give to any man, that you find such a person.
But strength comes from within, then you must find the strength to flourish and prosper for yourself. For that in and of itself, is the source of true salvation.
Do not harm or hate those who would seek to destroy you. There is no need, all you need to do is be the better you. With each passing day create a new and better you.
A better you, that can withstand the hate and return it with love.
Don't ask them to relent or repent, don't try to forgive or forget. Let them be who they are, but don't let them interfere with your ability to make your life better.

The true test of courage is the granting of beingness to those who would harm you.

An eye for an eye and a tooth for a tooth will do nothing but leave the world blind and toothless.

You will soon realize that those who are trying to harm you are nothing more than blind and toothless. They can't see and have no teeth. How can they truly harm you?

Let them rant and rave as you make a better you. Seek to flourish and prosper and you will win.

Looking Up

Feet, feet, feet.
All I see is feet.
Feet, feet, feet.
Everywhere I go,
Feet, feet, feet.
All I see is feet.
Feet, feet, feet.
Everyone is feet
One day I looked up and saw faces.

Rainbows

What is a fascination with rainbows?
Oh, I thought about that. Rainbows only happen during special conditions. Things must be just right for a rainbow to appear.
As our lives are so busy, we rarely get a chance to see a rainbow.
The same is true for the people in our lives.
Only during special conditions are the people around us so gracious and happy, and our lives so busy we tend to miss the rainbows that come from the people around us.
I am glad to say that a rainbow shines from my soul all the time these days. And with that rainbow in my heart people seem to notice what's going on for me.
Strangers who don't even know me will see my smile and the rainbow in my heart and ask, "Hi, how are you doing today?"
It is truly an amazing thing. My surprise turns to interest, and I will honestly ask them how they're doing and start a conversation.
It makes me glad that I can share the rainbow from within. In these dark and stormy times, it is wonderful to see a rainbow.

The Epiphany

An incident has taken place in my life that has caused me to reevaluate everything I have ever known, and everything I have ever felt. Looking at who I was, who I am now, and who I want to be. Oddly enough this is the second time in my life I have had such an epiphany.

The first time happened when I was very young, and that epiphany was, that I would win no matter the personal cost.

That certainly set me on a path and caused me to be a very gruff person. I discovered that I didn't like him very much.

The second life-changing event turned me into a person of love. I no longer feel the need to win.

Because to me, this connection I now have with people around me is more important.

I no longer feel the need to be better than anyone. The only person I must be better than is the person I was yesterday.

I have to keep reminding myself of this fact, not that I would revert to the gruff person, he has gone and never to return.

I remind myself because I want to push myself forward and be the best me, I can be.

The people around me deserve no less.

Forum Of Secrets

Soft, gentle, but mysterious because no one knows what I am like on the inside, but once you get to know me, you will understand that there is much more hidden inside.

I am like a puzzle: I intrigue and keep my distance, but for those who truly touch my heart, I will become the most open and devoted. I catch the moments of life; I believe in the magic of meetings. I want to get to know you, to see if we can share a wavelength.

Experiencing mutual understanding is so important to me. I'm really looking to connect with someone who can share understanding, no matter what life throws our way.

It means a lot to me to also be standing by her, ready to understand her perspective in every situation.

Walk out in the rain.

There are times when one must accept the reality of existence.
To see clearly what you can do, what you can be, and what you can have.
I took a walk today, there's a hilltop in the area that I go to.
I looked out for miles as I walked, and it started to rain.
Then I began to look at it like a gift. The rain started to wash away desires, upsets, problems and wants.
For the first time in a long while I saw with clarity who I was, what I needed to do, and what I could have.
None of those things were what I thought they were. Demons from my past were coming to haunt me. Yet, the rain washed it all away.
It's never that easy. The demons will return, and I will confront them, and handle them for good. For now, I'm happy with myself and who I am.

The Author

We are all the Author of the book of our lives.
As children, we learn to write stories.
As teenagers, we tried to rebel against those stories.
As young adults, we start to figure out what story we will write. Will it be a tragedy, a comedy, or a drama?
Too often people fail to understand that they are the author of their own story.
Look what you did to me. Look how bad my life is. This is how I will excuse my bad behavior.
It is only by accepting that you are the author of your own book that you will understand, that everything in your life is there because you wrote it on the pages of your life.
It is never too late to change a tragedy to a comedy. Life is to be enjoyed. It's never too late to change the drama to make you happy.
You are the author of your own book.
The pages that have been written cannot be changed. The empty Pages before you can be filled with whatever you feel is appropriate.
Understanding that you are the author of your own book will help you to see the only person that can harm you, is you. To write mean and hateful things, you will produce mean and hateful things in your life.
You are the source of your own problems.

It will not be easy, but you can change the direction of life by working on filling the empty Pages with love and compassion. You are the author of your own book, make it count.

The Roman Within

I feel that the Roman civilization has a lot to admire. They gave us art, architecture mythology, and ways of thinking, being, and doing that surpasses any civilization that came before it.

I have always felt like a Roman in some ways. These viewpoints have become part of me. As I have come to discover you can't have one without the other. The other being the wars, brutality, conquering and devastation.

On a personal note, I have to be careful of the Roman within. Being unchecked I have seen the swath of devastation left behind me. While I go to make up the damage, it is not quite fully repaired. Like a rip in your jacket, you can sew it up, but you still see the tear. Curb the Roman within. Stop the devastation before it starts. Hold onto the best parts while leaving the worst behind.

The Friend

There are times in your life when you meet someone so special they are not like any others you have met.

And then that moment you feel an overwhelming desire to be their friend.

This is the type of person who walks down The streets of the city is smiling at everyone they see.

They capture every moment to make the best of it, and when you're with them they make you feel like the most important person in the world.

They have their honor and their integrity. This is the type of person everyone strives to be like but doesn't always succeed.

A loving and giving individual. Who will be back in your time of need? And expect nothing in return.

I have a friend like that, and I wish I could be as good to them as they have been to me.

The Choice

There is a group of good people that I have been associated with, and I still feel that I'm not part of that group.
They are a group of good members, they have a righteous cause and are trying to do the best they can.
Yet still I feel that I am not part of them. I work with them I take care of their needs I make sure they have a place to do their work, but the feeling remains.
I have had the feeling for quite some time that I keep myself distanced from them because I don't want to be hurt emotionally, but is that really the case?
I know what their cause is, and it is just. I do not believe that any of these people could even harm me emotionally. So why is it that I can't feel like I'm part of the group?
Recent events and wonderful people have made me realize that I have not removed myself from the group because they will hurt me. The truth is, I am more concerned with hurting them.
So it comes down to this choice. Do I continue to stand back away from the group knowing that they are all good people, or do I embrace the group and pray that I can control myself and keep from hurting them.
I see now that I can harm them by keeping my distance. By not being cause over my environment, but being the effect of it, and being the effect will cause harm.

At least while I am embracing them I can have some measure of control that keeps the harm at bay.

I will fall, I will make mistakes. I will get back up, and choose to continue forward with the help of the people that I have around.

The choice, I choose to be cause over my environment and the people in it. To embrace the group and hope that we can keep each other from falling. And if we do, there are many around to help pick us back up.

Desires

Desire, the word itself dredges up all kinds of emotions. From the heights of elation to the depths of despair.

I believe that the word should be changed to goals. From the heights of elation, attainable goals. To the depths of despair, an unattainable goal.

Looking at it in this light, you will soon discover that there is no such thing as an unattainable goal.

There is no such thing as failure, there is only a lack of persistence.

But what does that have to do with desire?

To desire is, to long for, or to hope for something. So, to desire something is to never attain it.

However, goals are attainable. Never desire anything.

Make goals and plans and figure out how you can get what you want.

The Traffic

It's interesting as we get caught in traffic, all we see are cars. Big ones, little ones, fast ones, and slow ones. Red cars, blue cars, orange cars, purple cars, all moving at top speed in a direction. Whatever that top speed might be.

As I sat in traffic, I realized that all of these vehicles were being controlled by some person behind the wheel. Just like being in a body. Big people, small people, fast people, and slow people. They were all heading for their own destinations for their own reasons. And then a flash of insight came to mind. All of those people were spirits.

So, a spirit in a body, in a body. So, no wonder traffic is all kinds of crazy. :-)

Hi Smiley

Two weeks ago, I had someone ask about grumpy, meaning me. While I did not take offense at this, it did make me wonder. Is that how people view me?

Things had changed for me, and it was starting to show in my actions of how I was dealing with people.

Today I walked by a lady, and she smiled as if she was truly glad to see me. "Hi Smiley," she said as she went by.

This was a long way from grumpy, and I found that I was glad for it. I found that I liked it.

What was even more important was, I was happy that people were glad to have me around.

Maybe it's not so bad to be nice to people. I might even begin to enjoy it.

The Open Road.

I seem to remember the best time of my life was when I lived on the open road.

Living as a beggar, my life was free of responsibility. I had nowhere to be, and nothing to do, it was nothing but me and the open road.

I saw the beauty and majesty of the open sky. I would head out into the field and see the beauty of the night sky.

The Awesome wonder of the true Milky Way with no lights to interfere as the stars danced across the vestige.

The beauty of the Canyon is cut by a raging river. The beauty of architecture is built by men who praise their god.

Yet to me, the most amazing thing is the people I met. Some who I had a little more than I did, yet we're still willing to share.

As I walked across our beautiful land, It was the people that filled me with joy.

Some were very surprised at the attitude I had; I would take nothing without some kind of return. I worked for everything I got, not begging, but asking politely. Doing what needed to be done to get what I needed.

People expected little from a bum, and they were more than surprised at the job that I gave them in return.

Even though I was a bum, it gave me satisfaction to know that I could surprise and delight people.

Many of them wished me to stay and they could find me work or help me get a job. But the open road called and in short order, I was on my way.

The most interesting experience was dealing with an Indian tribe. I was never really sure which tribe they were, but it truly didn't matter.

They accepted me, not as a white man, but as a brother. It's the one place I stayed the longest, I was on a ranch helping with the horses when one of the tribal elders came to see me.

He wanted to talk to the white man who was on a soul quest. He said that he saw me for who I was, he said many things that made no sense, but when the time was right I would understand.

I continued on my journey and saw many beautiful places and many wonderful people. It was the most inspiring time in my life, Because I expected nothing from anyone. No one expected anything of me, and both sides were pleasantly surprised.

I went to see what I was fighting for. What I discovered was something that I would have sacrificed a lot more to preserve.

The Two Wolves.

This really isn't a poem, but it is a story that needs to be said.
It's funny, I pulled out the poem of the open road. It made me think about what that Indian Elder told me.
One of the things he told me about was the wolf, an animal with a Spirit of bravery, loyalty, and honor.
In this cave there were two wolves. One was a kind and loving wolf, and the other was fiercely protective and downright vicious. "They are both you," said the elder. You must choose which path to walk.
In confusion, I asked, "how do I choose?"
His answer was, "Which one will you feed?"
He would say no more on the subject, and I truly didn't understand what it meant at the time.
I now understand it's Time to feed the Wolf of love and compassion.

The Psychotic Babysitter

Bandit was an interesting dog.
I brought him over to a friend's house and they had just adopted a kitten named Fred.
At first, the two were not certain about each other.
Fred took a swipe at Bandit. He was not going to have that at all. So, he got on top of Fred and sat on his head.
Fred was not so happy about it. He squirmed his way out from under Bandit and ran off. Bandit chased Fred down and sat on the head again.
This went on for about half an hour with my friends laughing the whole time, after that, the two curled up together and went to sleep, it was so cute.
After that Bandit was named the psychotic babysitter.

The Thin Line

There is a thin line between good and evil. With a conflict in every man's heart between good and evil, justice and injustice.
Between what is needed, and what is desired. Men do not always win that conflict.
There are times when evil takes over. And good men must take up the challenge. to protect those who won't even go near that line.
Good people who are not willing to fight that fight. Good men must walk that line between good and evil.
Very few, that I have observed, can walk that line without falling over into the evil side.
To fight evil you must do evil deeds. It tears you apart, the things you must do to protect others fill you with self-doubt, self-loathing, and contempt of self. The trick is to walk that line without becoming evil.
To do those damn distasteful things without becoming the thing itself.
My only hope is that I can walk away from that line, with my honor intact.

The Mask We Wear

I must put on the face the world wants to see.
They can not know the real me. The soft good man would be chewed up by the world we know.
Time moves forward being battered by the onslaught of meanness, I forget that I was once a good man. The mask has become part of me.
In the deepest part of the night, alone I can see myself.
I become less of who I am and more of what the world demands of me.
It is time to rage against the world and take back myself.
remove the mask, with the power that I am demanding anyone to challenge my right to be who I am.

Who are you?

From time to time, I have asked the question of myself, who are you?

The question itself has no easy answer and perhaps that is the point. As we struggle to find out who we are now, it has become very pointed to me that the question itself is headed for the destination. Who are you? I am not the job title, that is what I do, not who I am. Still, who am I?

I am not my brother. I am not the father; I am not the son. They are only descriptions of some aspects of my life. Still, who am I?

They are not me. I came to realize that we have defined ourselves by what we are and are not. Still, who am I?

And for some by what emotions they show, I am not happy. I am sad. I am angry. Still, who am I?

I finally came to the conclusion that the answer was too simple, "I am" and that's all "I" need to be.

Embracing Life

It is interesting to note that from the time I was very young, I was never afraid of death. Somehow, I knew I was a spiritual being. To me, death was simply a matter of a transformation.

I am getting old, and as I look back on my life, I see that I was always running from death. I ran from death, I hid from death, I trick death, and I faced my own death more than once, but I have come to realize that I never truly embraced life. I fought for life in many ways, but I have never embraced life.

The road behind me is longer than the road ahead of me, and when my time comes I think I will be glad of it, but that will not stop me from fighting for every last second.

For now, in the season of winter I am beginning to embrace life. To allow people into my life and to accept them for who they are, not what I expect them to be.

Because now I understand that my biggest fear is not death, but of failure. I fought throughout my life to win, to be the best. To be someone who can be admired. The truth of the matter is, that I was trying to be interesting. What I understand now is that my biggest failure in life is that I was not interested.

Now, with whatever time I have left it is necessary for me to embrace life by being interested. Interested in those around me interested in things that I truly never cared for before. Being interesting has done nothing but make me a sad crusty old Man. An individuated individual who will not be a part of any group. For it is difficult to be part of the group when you are an 'only one.'

Transitions

Recent events have been instrumental in changing who I am.
The event was heartbreaking and soul-crushing, but I survived.
I had no idea how that happened because in fact, I didn't survive.
The man I was, is no longer the man I am now.
The man I was, was all kinds of nasty and mean. That attitude was necessary for him to survive.
I look now from the outside and see that man and feel pity for him.
He died that day, I do feel remorse. Yet, I don't regret that he's gone.
A new me was born that day. As this was a recent event I have no words to describe what happened yet.
What I do know, is that I feel more love for my fellow man. A Sense of wonderment that I could never feel before.
While there is still the hole of discontent of his passing, it is quickly being filled with connections of people that surround me.
Very few people around me even knew of the event, and none of them knew what was going on, as it was happening.
The choice was made, I decided to let him go, and I began a new life.

It’s a wonderful life

It's intriguing how Emotional growth unfolds through overcoming early struggles. have you ever Pondered how your childhood influences who you are today?

How do the dreams from your younger years shape your present ambitions? It did for me, for all the wrong reasons.

I would now like to be interested.

It makes me wonder what my life would’ve been like if I had learned these lessons earlier.

What would my life be like if I had learned to be interested instead of interesting when I was younger?

And how young would I have had to of been? Would it have changed my upbringing? Most of my life was spent being interesting, a selfish thing I know, but I did get to fulfill dreams of being a musician to being a comedian.

Had I just been interested would I still be a bodyguard? and if so, would that have led me to be a musician.

Would it have changed the way I interacted with my father? And if so, how?

I look at each step, each chapter along the way and wonder what would’ve happened if I had been interested.

Would I be in the same place I am now? And the answer is emphatically no.

I had to be who I was to be in a position to learn the lesson that is now the most important thing to me. To be interested.

The Wish

If I was given three wishes by a genie in a magic lamp, I would only need one.

I would not wish for riches or fame, for those I can get myself.

Those, l can get myself with my ability.

Honestly what I would wish for is to be a better me. To make my life a life of giving and caring to make whoever I'm with the happiest woman in the world.

To feel their joy and contentment as I walk into the room and know that it's genuine honest and real.

To be able to talk to people and truly be interested in who and what they are.

To find out who the core being is, protect it, and help them in any way I can.

To be able to have a communication with anyone anywhere at any time Without trying to make them feel like I'm better than they are.

To truly humble myself so that others would share with me some of their deepest thoughts most terrible fears and genuine desires.

And be the type of person that would understand those thoughts allay those fears and help them achieve their desires.

That is what a true man is, it is my deepest wish that I can become that man.

The Flower

For so long the seed has sat dormant. Recently the plant of my soul has begun to grow.

It was tended by a loving gardener who wanted to see the sprout and growth of this man.

It was odd that the plant of love could grow from the ground of anger and hate.

With frustration, the gardener never gave up on the job, taking great care as the plant grew.

The larger it became the less frustrating it was as more love was taking control over the little plant.

One day excitement filled the Gardener. A flower bud was starting to appear.

With extra special care, the gardener tended to the plant.

Amazingly the bud turned into a beautiful flower. One of love, care, and compassion.

Joy

Joy is multiplied when shared, and I am sending a portion of happiness and fortune your way, carried by my smile! Please inform me upon its arrival ... Alright?

rthomasmcpherson@gmail.com

Don't miss out!

Visit the website below and you can sign up to receive emails whenever R Thomas McPherson publishes a new book. There's no charge and no obligation.

https://books2read.com/r/B-A-JSVG-KFZKF

Did you love *To Flourish and Prosper.*? Then you should read *Investigation*[1] by R Thomas McPherson!

[2]

Anteagen, the home world of the Wilson Corporation. Rick remembered the history lesson. This world was a new beginning for the Wilson corp. This was the first habitable planet that Jeb Wilson discovered. The Corporation had been roaming the galaxy for thirty years, after leaving earth. Once they found this planet, it was the promise land. A place to put down roots and expand the population.

There were areas of green fertile land with enough water on the planet to make a new start. In the beginning there was peace and plenty. Other worlds were found and colonized but none were as

1. https://books2read.com/u/bPQPRJ

2. https://books2read.com/u/bPQPRJ

lovely as Anteagen. That is why The Wilson Corporate based their headquarters here.

The problem was that man brought his hostile nature with him. After three hundred years the grotesqueries of human nature started to show itself again. That's where Rick came in. Rick Thompson an investigator for the Wilson Corporation is set on a case that leads him though action and adventure.

Also by R Thomas McPherson

The Corporate Wars

Investigation

Insurrection

The Corporate Wars Vol 2

Inquisition

Inclusion

Incursion

Invasion

The Veterans of the Psychic Wars

Hostile Waters

Third Dawn

Identity Crisis

War Drums

Battle Cry

Queen's Gambit

Standalone

The Wastelands
The Corporate Wars
The Veterans of the Psychic Wars
The Veterans of the Psychic Wars Volume 2
To Flourish and Prosper.

www.ingramcontent.com/pod-product-compliance
Lightning Source LLC
LaVergne TN
LVHW090128160826
845673LV00015B/1119

* 9 7 9 8 2 3 0 0 0 3 9 9 1 *